piano I vocal I guitar

destiny's child | the writing's on the wall

Visit Hal Leonard Online at
www.halleonard.com

ISBN 0-634-02913-4

7777 W. BLUEMOUND RD. P.O. BOX 13819 MILWAUKEE, WI 53213

Visit Hal Leonard Online at
www.halleonard.com

destiny's child | the writing's on the wall

THE INTRO

Words and Music by BEYONCE KNOWLES,
KELENDRIA ROWLAND, LaTAVIA ROBERSON
and LeTOYA LUCKETT

SO GOOD

Words and Music by KANDI L. BURRUSS,
KEVIN BRIGGS, BEYONCE KNOWLES,
KELENDRIA ROWLAND, LaTAVIA ROBERSON
and LaTOYA LUCKETT

BILLS, BILLS, BILLS

Words and Music by KANDI L. BURRUSS,
KEVIN BRIGGS, BEYONCE KNOWLES,
KELENDRIA ROWLAND and LeTOYA LUCKETT

At first we start-ed out real cool,
Now you've been max-in' out my card,

tak-in' me plac-es I had nev-er ___ been. ___ But now ___
gave me bad cred-it, buy me gifts with ___ my ___ own name.

CONFESSIONS

Words and Music by MELISSA ELLIOTT,
GERARD THOMAS and DONALD HOLMES

BUG A BOO

Words and Music by KANDI L. BURRUSS,
KEVIN BRIGGS, BEYONCE KNOWLES, KELENDRIA ROWLAND,
LaTAVIA ROBERSON and LeTOYA LUCKETT

Steadily, half-time feel

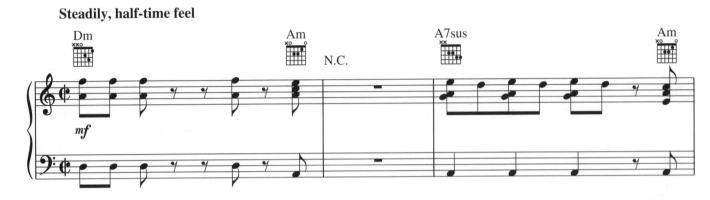

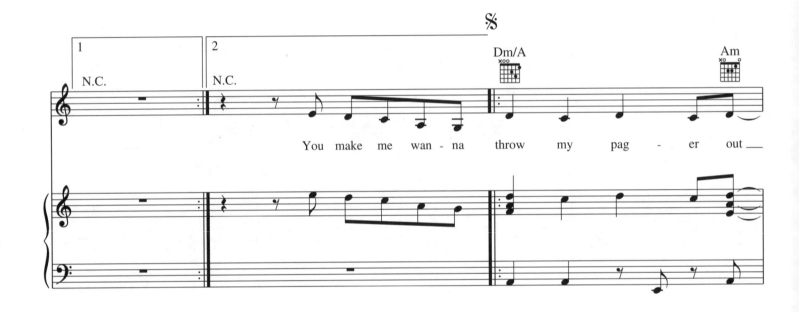

You make me wan-na throw my pag-er out ___ the win-dow, tell ___ M - C - I to cut ___ the phone poles, break ___

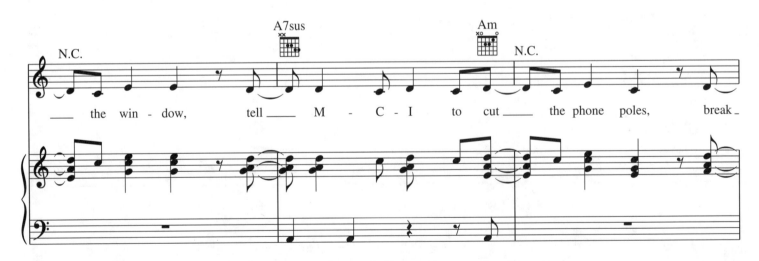

Original key: Ab minor. This edition has been transposed up one half-step to be more playable.

TEMPTATION

Words and Music by BEYONCE KNOWLES,
KELENDRIA ROWLAND, LaTAVIA ROBERSON,
LeTOYA LUCKETT, DWAYNE WIGGINS,
CARL WHEELER and ANTHONY RAY

Moderately slow, in 2

I know you see me watch-ing you, and I see you watch-ing me, 'cause boy, your bod-y's call-ing; the temp-ta-tion is kill-ing me. I know you see me watch-ing you, and I see you watch-ing me, 'cause boy, your bod-y's call-ing; the temp-ta-tion is kill-ing me. I ta-tion is kill-ing me. I'm

Original key: Eb minor. This edition has been transposed up one half-step to be more playable.

CODA

NOW THAT SHE'S GONE

Words and Music by KENNETH FAMBRO,
DONYELL BOYNTON, TARA GETER,
LATRELLE SIMMONS and ELISE SIMMONS

CODA

WHERE DID YOU GO

Words and Music by BEYONCE KNOWLES,
KELENDRIA ROWLAND, LaTAVIA ROBERSON,
LeTOYA LUCKETT, PLATINUM STATUS
and CHRIS STOKES

Moderately

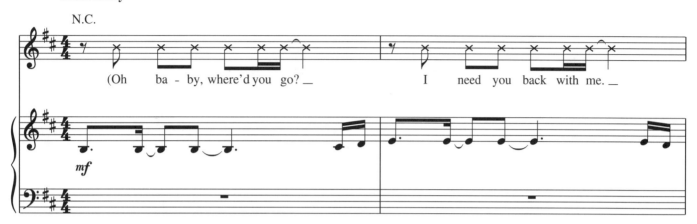

(Oh ba-by, where'd you go? __ I need you back with me. __

Oh ba-by, where'd you go? __ I need you back with me. __ Uh.)

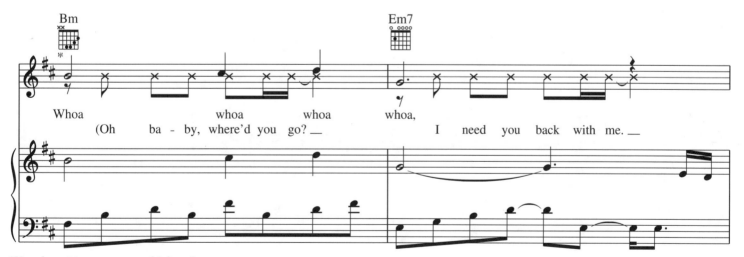

Whoa whoa whoa whoa, (Oh ba-by, where'd you go? __ I need you back with me. __

Vocals written one octave higher than sung.

HEY LADIES

Words and Music by KANDI L. BURRUSS,
KEVIN BRIGGS, BEYONCE KNOWLES,
KELENDRIA ROWLAND, LaTAVIA ROBERSON
and LaTOYA LUCKETT

*Vocals sung an octave lower

IF YOU LEAVE

Words and Music by T. TURMAN, R.L. HUGGER,
C. ELLIOT and O. HUNTER

*Vocals written one octave higher than sung.

JUMPIN, JUMPIN

Words and Music by BEYONCE KNOWLES,
RUFUS MOORE and CHAD MOORE

Moderately

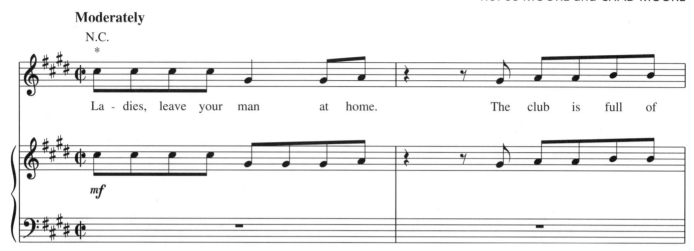

Ladies, leave your man at home. The club is full of

ballers and their pockets full grown. And all you fellas, leave your girl with her friends,

'cause it's eleven thirty, and the club is jumpin', jumpin'.

*Vocals sung an octave lower

* Lead vocal part sung second time only.

*Lead vocal part sung both times.

SAY MY NAME

Words and Music by RODNEY JERKINS,
LaSHAWN DANIELS, FRED JERKINS,
BEYONCE KNOWLES, KELENDRIA ROWLAND,
LaTAVIA ROBERSON and LeTOYA LUCKETT

SHE CAN'T LOVE YOU

Words and Music by KANDI L. BURRUSS,
KEVIN BRIGGS, BEYONCE KNOWLES,
KELENDRIA ROWLAND, LaTAVIA ROBERSON,
LaTOYA LUCKETT and INDIA LINDO

*Vocals sung an octave lower

STAY

Words and Music by
DARYL SIMMONS

Moderately

Ba - by, I want for no - thing, _ just _____ your ten-der, sweet lov - ing. _____ I know you've got _ your things _ to do, but

Vocals sung an octave lower

SWEET SIXTEEN

Words and Music by BEYONCE KNOWLES, KELENDRIA ROWLAND,
DWAYNE WIGGINS and JODY WATLEY

*Vocals sung an octave lower

THE OUTRO

Words and Music by
BEYONCE KNOWLES

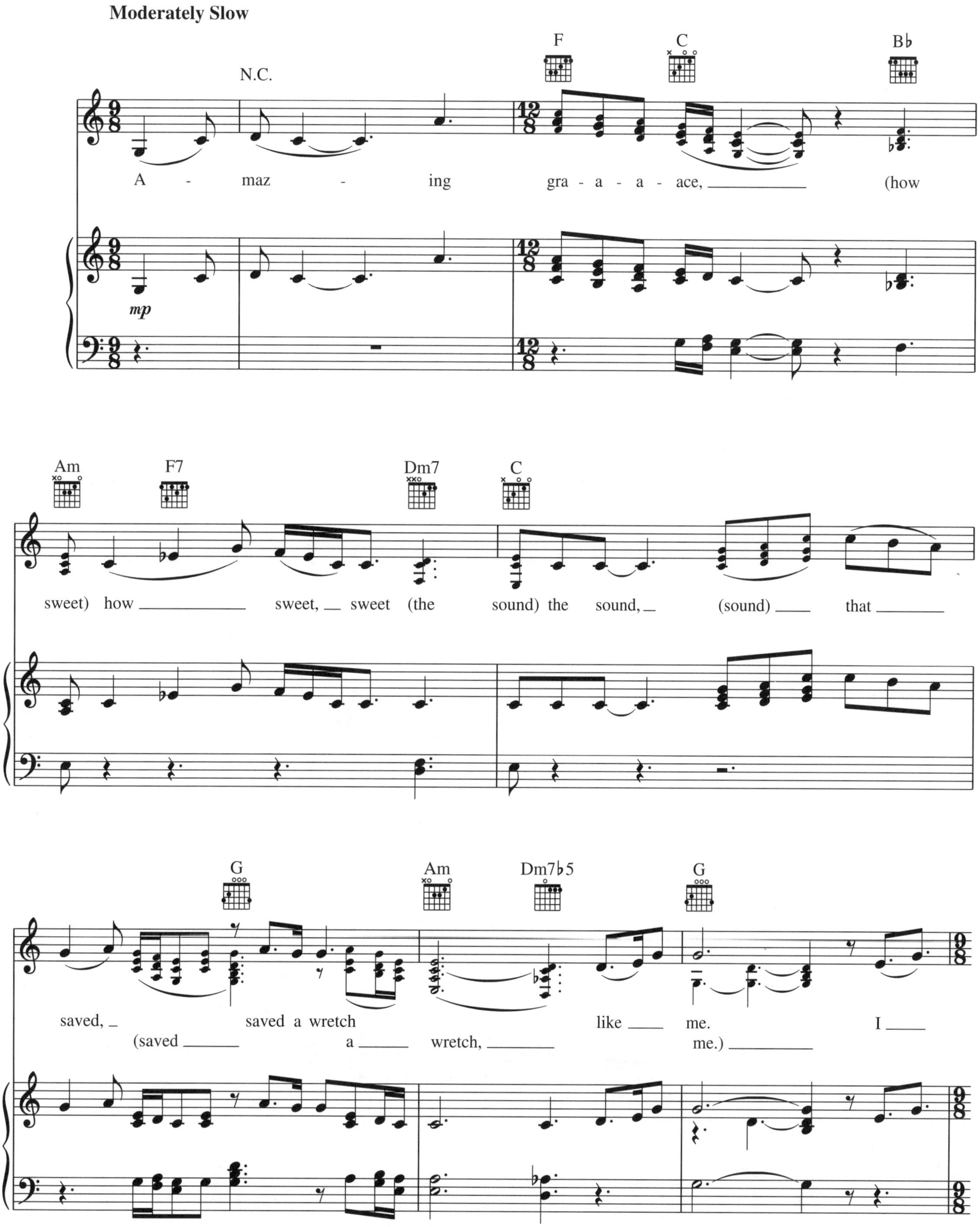